WIND ENERGY

PUTTING THE AIR TO WORK

JESSIE ALKIRE

Consulting Editor, Diane Craig, M.A./Reading Specialist

Super Sandcastle

An Imprint of Abdo Publishing
abdopublishing.com

abdopublishing.com

Published by Abdo Publishing, a division of ABDO, PO Box 398166, Minneapolis, Minnesota 55439. Copyright © 2019 by Abdo Consulting Group, Inc. International copyrights reserved in all countries. No part of this book may be reproduced in any form without written permission from the publisher. Super SandCastle™ is a trademark and logo of Abdo Publishing.

Printed in the United States of America, North Mankato, Minnesota

052018
092018

THIS BOOK CONTAINS
RECYCLED MATERIALS

Design and Production: Mighty Media, Inc.
Editor: Megan Borgert-Spaniol
Cover Photographs: Shutterstock; Wikimedia Commons
Interior Photographs: Crotched Mountain Foundation; iStockphoto; Mighty Media, Inc.; Shutterstock; Wikimedia Commons

Library of Congress Control Number: 2017961861

Publisher's Cataloging-in-Publication Data
Names: Alkire, Jessie, author.
Title: Wind energy: Putting the air to work / by Jessie Alkire.
Other titles: Putting the air to work
Description: Minneapolis, Minnesota : Abdo Publishing, 2019. | Series: Earth's
    energy innovations
Identifiers: ISBN 9781532115769 (lib.bdg.) | ISBN 9781532156489 (ebook)
Subjects: LCSH: Wind power--Juvenile literature. | Power resources--Juvenile
    literature. | Energy development--Juvenile literature. | Energy conversion--
    Juvenile literature.
Classification: DDC 333.92--dc23

Super SandCastle™ books are created by a team of professional educators, reading specialists, and content developers around five essential components—phonemic awareness, phonics, vocabulary, text comprehension, and fluency—to assist young readers as they develop reading skills and strategies and increase their general knowledge. All books are written, reviewed, and leveled for guided reading, early reading intervention, and Accelerated Reader™ programs for use in shared, guided, and independent reading and writing activities to support a balanced approach to literacy instruction.

CONTENTS

WHAT IS WIND ENERGY?

Wind energy is energy created by the air. Air moves through Earth's atmosphere. This motion is wind. Wind energy can be captured. It is used to make electricity.

Wind is a clean energy **resource**. It does not produce pollution. Wind is also renewable. It will never run out!

Wind turbine

Air has weight that puts pressure on Earth. Air flows from areas of high pressure to areas of low pressure. This is what causes wind.

ENERGY TIMELINE

500-900 CE

Persians use **windmills** to grind grain and pump water.

1887

The first electricity-producing wind **turbine** is built in Scotland.

1888

Charles F. Brush completes the first **automatic** wind turbine.

Discover how wind energy has changed over time!

1970s

Oil shortages spark greater interest in wind energy.

1980

The first **wind farm** is built in New Hampshire.

2000

The United States has nearly 100 wind farms.

EARLY WIND POWER

Wind energy has moved boats since ancient times. Persians used **windmills** by 900 CE. The mills could pump water and grind grain. Windmills later appeared around the world.

The first electricity-producing wind **turbine** was built in 1887. It was in Scotland. Charles Brush finished building an **automatic** wind turbine the next year.

Brush's automatic wind turbine

CHARLES F. BRUSH

BORN: March 17, 1849, Euclid, Ohio

DIED: June 15, 1929, Cleveland, Ohio

Charles F. Brush was an American inventor. He completed the first **automatic** wind **turbine** in 1888. The turbine was 60 feet (18 m) tall. It weighed 80,000 pounds (36,300 kg). And it used 144 blades! Brush used the turbine to power his Cleveland home.

WIND FARMS

Oil was a common energy **resource** in the 1900s. But there were shortages in the 1970s. Oil costs went up. Nations took greater interest in wind energy.

The first **wind farm** was built in New Hampshire in 1980. It had 20 **turbines**. There were nearly 100 US wind farms by 2000.

World's first wind farm in New Hampshire

Today's wind farms can be made up of hundreds of turbines.

CLEAN ENERGY

Wind energy is used around the world today. China is a top producer of wind power. So is the United States.

Wind energy costs are going down. They are closer to the costs of **fossil fuels**. But fossil fuels produce **greenhouse gases**. Using wind energy reduces this pollution.

Wind farm in China

Wind farms are often located on land that is also used for agriculture.

13

WIND POWER

Wind energy is mainly used to make electricity. This is done with **turbines**. Turbines are built on land or offshore. Offshore turbines receive strong winds. They could power large coastal cities!

Smaller turbines are also used. They can power single homes. They also power water systems, **batteries**, and more.

Small wind turbines

Offshore wind farms are common in northern European countries such as Denmark.

TURBINES

Most wind **turbines** have three blades. The blades are attached to a tower. Towers usually reach more than 100 feet (30 m) tall. This lets turbines capture faster winds.

Some turbines rotate around a **vertical** axis. But most rotate around a **horizontal** axis. These turbines look like giant fans.

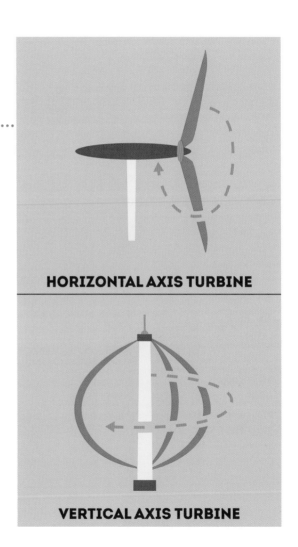

HORIZONTAL AXIS TURBINE

VERTICAL AXIS TURBINE

Thousands of birds and bats are killed each year by wind turbines. Vertical axis turbines are thought to be safer for wildlife.

SPINNING ELECTRICITY

The blades of a **turbine** are attached to a rotor. Wind turns the blades and rotor. The rotor is connected to a shaft. The shaft spins a **generator**. The spinning creates electricity.

The turbines on one **wind farm** can power thousands of homes and businesses!

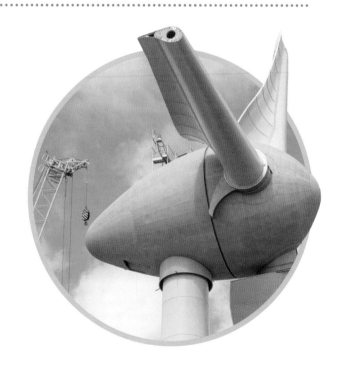

Wind turbine rotor

INSIDE A WIND TURBINE

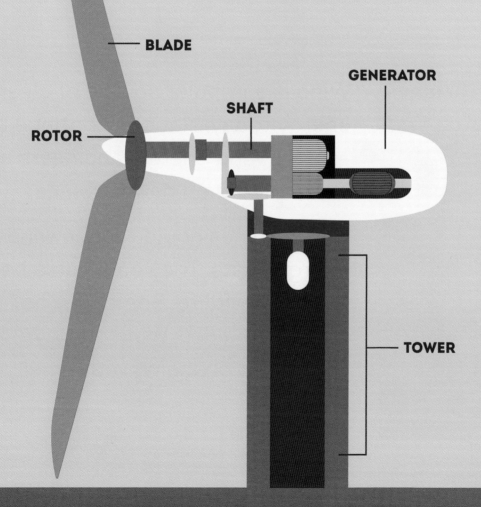

BLADE

GENERATOR

SHAFT

ROTOR

TOWER

WINDS OF CHANGE

Offshore wind farm construction

Wind is a popular source of clean energy today. Nations continue to explore wind energy. Engineers are also working on new **turbines**.

New turbines could reduce wind energy costs. They could also be safer for wildlife. Some may not even use blades. Wind energy tools keep changing with time!

Wind farm in Spain, a leading country in wind power production

MORE ABOUT WIND ENERGY

Do you want to tell others about wind energy? Here are some fun facts to share!

WIND TURBINES can have as many as 8,000 different parts!

THE FIRST US OFFSHORE WIND FARM was built in Rhode Island in 2016.

THE LARGEST wind **turbine** blades are 290 feet (88 m) long.

TEST YOUR KNOWLEDGE

1. Who invented the first **automatic** wind **turbine**?

2. When was the first **wind farm** built?

3. Most turbines have four blades. **TRUE OR FALSE?**

THINK ABOUT IT!

Sailboats and kites use wind energy. How else can you use wind energy?

ANSWERS: 1. Charles F. Brush 2. 1980 3. False

GLOSSARY

automatic – moving or acting by itself.

battery – a small container filled with chemicals that makes electrical power.

fossil fuel – a fuel formed from the remains of plants or animals. Coal, oil, and natural gas are fossil fuels.

generator – a machine that creates electricity.

greenhouse gas – a gas, such as carbon dioxide, that traps heat in Earth's atmosphere.

horizontal – in the same direction as the ground, or side to side.

resource – something that is usable or valuable.

turbine – a machine that produces power when it is rotated at high speed.

vertical – in the opposite direction from the ground, or up-and-down.

wind farm – an area where there are many wind turbines.

windmill – a machine that uses wind energy to do physical work.